Bible reflections
for older people

BRF

The Bible Reading Fellowship
15 The Chambers, Vineyard
Abingdon OX14 3FE
brf.org.uk

The Bible Reading Fellowship (BRF) is a Registered Charity (233280)

ISBN 978 0 85746 909 0

Acknowledgements
Scripture quotations marked with the following acronyms are taken from the version shown. Where no acronym is given, the quotation is taken from the same version as the headline reference. **NIV** or **NIV 1984**: The Holy Bible, New International Version (Anglicised edition) copyright © 1979, 1984, 2011 by Biblica. Used by permission of Hodder & Stoughton Publishers, a Hachette UK company. All rights reserved. 'NIV' is a registered trademark of Biblica. UK trademark number 1448790. **ESV**: The Holy Bible, English Standard Version, published by HarperCollins Publishers, © 2001 Crossway Bibles, a division of Good News Publishers. Used by permission. All rights reserved. **KJV**: The Authorised Version of the Bible (The King James Bible), the rights in which are vested in the Crown, are reproduced by permission of the Crown's Patentee, Cambridge University Press.

Article and photo on pages 35–36 reproduced by kind permission of *Woman Alive* and Angela Lucas.

Every effort has been made to trace and contact copyright owners for material used in this resource. We apologise for any inadvertent omissions or errors, and would ask those concerned to contact us so that full acknowledgement can be made in the future.

A catalogue record for this book is available from the British Library

Printed and bound in the UK by Zenith Media NP4 0DQ

Contents

About the writers

Tony Horsfall is a freelance trainer and retreat leader based in Yorkshire. His BRF books include *Resilience in Life and Faith* (2019, with Debbie Hawker), *Servant Ministry* (second edition, 2019), *Spiritual Growth in a Time of Change* (2016) and *Rhythms of Grace* (2012). He also contributes to BRF Bible reading notes *New Daylight*. Married to Evelyn, they have two children and four grandchildren.

Sue Richards won *The Upper Room* writing competition in 2017. She lives in Newport Pagnell with her husband and son and has personal experience of caring for disabled members of her family. She teaches Functional Skills English to adults and has written for a wide variety of magazines and anthologies. She also serves as a deacon in her church and an electoral canvasser.

Roger Combes was a vicar in Hastings for 17 years after serving parishes in London and Cambridge. Before retiring, he served as an archdeacon in West Sussex. He and his wife live in Crawley. He has been a supporter of Bournemouth Football Club for 60 years, and still finds it slightly unbelievable that they are now playing in the Premier League.

'Tricia Williams is a freelance writer and editor, with a passion for helping people engage with God's word. She has a special interest in providing spiritual support for people living with dementia and has recently completed research in this area. 'Tricia is married to Emlyn (also a writer for *Bible Reflections for Older People*), and they have two adult children.

From the Editor

Welcome to this new collection of Bible reflections.

I moved into my first flat with a garden – as opposed to a gravel patch – towards the end of July 2003. This was too late in the year to experience the explosion of green that comes with the warmth of late spring, so I was taken by surprise the following year. The clouds of new growth were spectacular, and they were a constant reminder of one of my favourite lines in one of my favourite poems: 'Who would have thought my shrivelled heart / Could have recovered greenness?', from 'The Flower' by George Herbert.

Research published last year showed that just 20 minutes, three times a week, spent 'sitting or walking in a place that provides you with a sense of nature' has a measurable effect on well-being: lowering heart rate, blood pressure and cortisol levels, and lifting mood.* This is one of the reasons I try to get my dad out into the beautifully kept garden of his care home as often as the weather allows. Even if he's reluctant at first, he always feels better as soon as we get outside, and so do I.

I hope you enjoy this new edition of *Bible Reflections for Older People* through the months of late spring and summer. I hope it will help you rest a while in green pastures and feed your soul.

God bless you

Eley
x

* Research by the University of Michigan, published
  in *Frontiers in Psychology*, April 2019.

Using these reflections

Perhaps you have always had a special daily time for reading the Bible and praying. But now, as you grow older, you are finding it more difficult to keep to a regular pattern or find it hard to concentrate. Or maybe you've never done this before. Whatever your situation, these Bible reflections aim to help you take a few moments to read God's word and pray, whenever you have time or feel that would be helpful.

When to read them

You may find it helpful to use these Bible reflections in the morning or last thing at night, or any time during the day. There are 40 daily reflections here, grouped around four themes. Each one includes some verses from the Bible, a reflection to help you in your own thinking about God, and a prayer suggestion. The reflections aren't dated, so it doesn't matter if you don't want to read every day. The Bible verses are printed, but if you'd like to read from your own Bible that's fine too.

How to read them

- **Take time** to quieten yourself, becoming aware of God's presence, asking him to speak to you through the Bible and the reflection.

- **Read** the Bible verses and the reflection:
  - What do you especially like or find helpful in these verses?
  - What might God be saying to you through this reading?
  - Is there something to pray about or thank God for?

- **Pray**. Each reflection includes a prayer suggestion. You might like to pray for yourself or take the opportunity to think about and pray for others.

The shepherd psalm

Tony Horsfall

Is there any passage of scripture more well known or more greatly loved than Psalm 23? I don't think so. Its beautiful words have inspired and encouraged God's people since it was penned so long ago by King David.

Why is it still so popular? I think it's because it is such a positive psalm, packed full of reassurance about the love, care and protection of God for his people. That's why people love to sing it, whether at a wedding (starting a new life together) or at a funeral (as life comes to a close), and at all points in-between (expressing our faith and trust in God).

The danger, of course, is that we may be over-familiar with its message, so as you read it again, ask that God will speak to you afresh through its inspired words. In the next few days, we will meditate on different themes that arise naturally from the text, each one bringing particular encouragement to us. These are timeless truths. With God as our shepherd, we will lack for nothing. With him beside us, we need have no fear.

Psalm 23:1; Acts 17:22a–23 (NIV 1984)

Relationship

The Lord is my shepherd, I shall not be in want.

[Paul said,] 'Men of Athens! I see that in every way you are very religious. For as I walked around and looked carefully at your objects of worship, I even found an altar with this inscription: to an unknown god. Now what you worship as something unknown I am going to proclaim to you.'

Even as a boy, David was aware of God's presence. Out on the hillsides caring for the sheep, he discovered for himself the reality of knowing God. He discovered that God could be trusted to take care of him, helping him to protect his flock when bears or lions were on the prowl. He began to realise that God was like a shepherd to him, a God who would protect him and care for him. Over the years, David grew in this relationship and could confidently say, 'The Lord is my shepherd.'

Psalm 23 teaches us that it is possible for each of us to know God in a personal way. We do not have to live, like the people in Athens, with a vague notion of a god who is out there somewhere but impossible to know. Jesus, the good shepherd, laid down his life for us so that we could be brought into a relationship with God.

Don't be satisfied with anything less. God wants you to know him, and he wants to be your shepherd too.

■ PRAYER
Loving Lord, thank you that you are the good shepherd. Help me to know you more fully day by day. Amen

Psalm 23:2; Philippians 4:12b–13 (NIV 1984)

Contentment

He makes me lie down in green pastures, he leads me beside quiet waters.

I have learned the secret of being content in any and every situation, whether well fed or hungry, whether living in plenty or in want. I can do everything through him who gives me strength.

What is the secret of happiness in old age? I believe it is to discover the secret of contentment.

A good shepherd takes pride in caring for the sheep. He wants to provide them with lush pasture on which they can feed and graze. He seeks out fresh water, so they can drink and not be thirsty. His joy is to see them lying down, relaxed and at peace.

This beautiful picture reminds us that God wants us to be content. So often we feel restless and dissatisfied, frustrated with ourselves and unhappy in our circumstances. That's when we need to remind ourselves of all that is good in our lives and be thankful to God for what we do enjoy, rather than complaining about what we don't have.

As Paul discovered, being content is a choice we make. We choose to focus on the positive rather than the negative. We aim to be grateful rather than to grumble. As we do this, we find peace in our hearts, and we can rest contentedly.

Ask the good shepherd to bring you to that place of contentment.

■ PRAYER

Dear God, please give me the gift of contentment in all circumstances. Amen

Psalm 23:3a; 2 Corinthians 4:16 (NIV 1984)

Renewal

He restores my soul.

Therefore we do not lose heart. Though outwardly we are wasting away, yet inwardly we are being renewed day by day.

By the time you read this, I will be in my 70th year. I never thought when I was a young man that I would ever be this old, but here I am. I'm grateful for good heath, but like everyone else I have aches and pains, and I sometimes worry in case it's something sinister.

Ageing is never easy. For some, there are multiple health issues to face, as well as mental and emotional challenges. We quickly become aware of our human weakness and frailty. That's why the reminder from Psalm 23 today is so important. Our bodies may be getting weaker, but our inner lives can be getting stronger.

What does this mean in practice? It means that even as our physical and mental capacities may decline, our soul can still experience God's love and presence. We can be strengthened within and, despite our difficulties, still know joy and peace. With the shepherd's help, our faith can remain robust and healthy.

The best way to receive this inner renewal is to rest contentedly in God's presence. Picture yourself like a sheep lying down in those green pastures and beside the still waters, under the watchful eye of the shepherd. Don't rush away. Linger for a while and bask in God's acceptance of you. Feel the grip of grace upon your life.

■ **PRAYER**

Loving God, help me to rest in your presence. Amen

Psalm 23:3b; Isaiah 30:21 (NIV 1984)

Guidance

He guides me in paths of righteousness for his name's sake.

Whether you turn to the right or to the left, your ears will hear a voice behind you, saying, 'This is the way; walk in it.'

Life can be very perplexing. There are so many decisions to make and so many choices before us. How do we know what to do? How can we be sure that we are doing the right thing? Perhaps we were once very confident in our decision-making, but now as we get older we may be less certain and more easily confused.

We are reminded in Psalm 23 that our good shepherd is there to guide us. He wants to help us find the right path and walk in his ways. A primary response is to pray about things and to ask God to lead us. Being prayerful about every aspect of our lives is a simple but vital part in making good decisions.

Having done that, we can then listen for the voice of God, either through scripture or within ourselves. God is able to speak to us, and as his sheep we are able to recognise the shepherd's voice. For me, this mostly comes as a sense of peace. When I consider any course of action, I look for this peace to be in my heart. If I have no peace, I don't proceed. If I have peace, then I assume that is the way to go.

■ **PRAYER**

Loving God, help me always to recognise your voice amid the noise and distractions of the world. Amen

Psalm 23:4a; Matthew 1:22–23 (NIV 1984)

Presence

Even though I walk through the valley of the shadow of death, I will fear no evil, for you are with me.

All this took place to fulfil what the Lord had said through the prophet: 'The virgin will be with child and will give birth to a son, and they will call him Immanuel' – which means, 'God is with us.'

A friend was diagnosed with an aggressive form of breast cancer, which required radical surgery. Leading up to the operation, she had been fine, buoyed by the prayers of her friends and family, but as she waited for surgery, she had a panic attack. All she could think to do was to breathe deeply and slowly and to repeat aloud to herself, 'God is with us. God is with us.'

At that moment, she heard voices in the next cubicle. The doctor was introducing himself to the patient. 'Hello,' he said, 'my name is Dr Emmanuel, and my name means "God is with us".' It was an amazing moment of confirmation that God was truly with my friend in her time of need. This incident instilled in her a sense of God's presence that calmed her fears and carried her through the long weeks of treatment still ahead of her.

The psalmist also reminds us that in the darkest valley, God is with us, and we need not be afraid. Whatever you are facing today, say with confidence, 'God is with me. God is with me.'

■ **PRAYER**

Dear God, thank you that you are with me – Immanuel – wherever I am, whatever the challenges that face me. Amen

Psalm 23:4b; 2 Corinthians 1:3–4 (NIV 1984)

Comfort

Your rod and your staff, they comfort me.

Praise be to the God and Father of our Lord Jesus Christ, the Father of compassion and the God of all comfort, who comforts us in all our troubles, so that we can comfort those in any trouble with the comfort we ourselves have received from God.

Psalm 23 makes clear to us that we cannot expect life to be easy. On our journey through life, we can expect there to be deep valleys and moments of darkness and fear. This realistic approach is far healthier than imagining that having faith in God will ensure we have no troubles. Even when we know God is leading us, we may sometimes find ourselves in hard places.

The good news is that even there, the ever-present God, who will never leave us or forsake us, will reassure and comfort us. The shepherd uses his rod to chase away wild animals that may attack the flock. With it, he protects his sheep. His staff is used to gently tap them on the shoulder, reminding them that he is there, or occasionally to pull them out of difficulty when they have fallen into danger.

The apostle Paul often found himself in difficulty, but he discovered at such times that God was able to comfort him. Furthermore, having experienced God's comfort himself, he found that he was able to comfort others from his own experience.

■ **PRAYER**
Loving God, may I know the reassuring tap of your staff on my shoulder today. Amen

Psalm 23:5a; Ephesians 1:3 (NIV 1984)

Supply

You prepare a table before me in the presence of my enemies.

Praise be to the God and Father of our Lord Jesus Christ, who has blessed us in the heavenly realms with every spiritual blessing in Christ.

The shepherd who appears in Psalm 23 is also a king, and now the picture changes from shepherd and sheep to a king and his subjects. The shepherd-king graciously invites us to join him at his banqueting table. As we can imagine, the table is creaking under the weight of his provision for us. Every delicacy we could ever desire is set before us, and we are free to enjoy his lavish hospitality.

I cannot read this verse without thinking of the Communion table. There, we see set before us the bread and the wine, symbols of the body and blood of Jesus and reminders of his amazing sacrifice on our behalf. Through his death, we are reconciled to God and become heirs of all the riches of God. Every time we share in Communion, we are sitting at the king's table. There is nothing that Satan, our enemy, can do to prevent us from receiving the blessing of God.

Today, you are invited to come and take your seat and receive from God whatever you need – forgiveness and pardon, grace and strength, healing and wholeness, peace and joy, and so on. All has been made freely available to us through Christ.

■ PRAYER

Loving God, thank you that you invite us to your banqueting table and provide so generously for our deepest needs. Amen

Psalm 23:5b; John 15:11 (NIV 1984)

Joy

You anoint my head with oil; my cup overflows.

[Jesus said,] 'I have told you this so that my joy may be in you and that your joy may be complete.'

The shepherd-king is our generous host. Not only has he prepared a lavish feast for us to enjoy, but he also welcomes us with tokens of his love and affection. He anoints his guests with oil, sweet-smelling perfumes signifying acceptance and esteem. Then he fills their cups with the finest wine, so full that they overflow – a clear demonstration of his generosity and free-flowing hospitality. Both images speak to us about the gift of the Holy Spirit, through whom the blessings of God are communicated to us. In particular, the anointing and the overflowing cup speak to us about the joy of the Lord, which he imparts to us.

Joy is one of the fruit of the Spirit (Galatians 5:22) and was a characteristic of the life of Jesus. He was a joyful person, who was good to be around and whose presence brought fun and laughter. That is why he wanted to share his joy with his disciples. This heavenly joy is not a matter of temperament, but is a gift from God. It is dependent not on happy circumstances but on the work of the Holy Spirit within us. The Bible knows nothing of a joyless Christianity. We are not called to be serious and sombre, but joyful and light-hearted.

■ PRAYER

Give me joy in my heart, keeping me praising,
give me joy in my heart, I pray;
give me joy in my heart, keep me praising,
keep me praising till the break of day.* Amen

* Popular hymn, author unknown.

Psalm 23:6a; Psalm 103:1-2 (NIV 1984)

Goodness

Surely goodness and love will follow me all the days of my life.

Praise the Lord, O my soul; all my inmost being, praise his holy name. Praise the Lord, O my soul, and forget not all his benefits.

I have often said that if ever I write an autobiography I will call it 'All the days of my life', using the words from this verse in Psalm 23.

Looking back over our lives and reflecting on the key moments is actually a very helpful thing to do, not simply because of nostalgia, but also to remind ourselves of the goodness of God. Many things are best seen with hindsight. Often, events we thought had gone wrong turn out to have been for the best. With a backwards glance, we can see how the providence of God has shaped circumstances for our good, even though they may have been painful at the time. All of this helps us to appreciate the goodness of God in its many and varied expressions. As you ponder this, what examples from your own story come to mind?

This reminder of past goodness is a great encouragement when we face an uncertain future. The God who is faithful, and has been faithful, will continue to be faithful, no matter what. As the hymn writer says, 'We'll praise him for all that is past and trust him for all that's to come.'*

■ PRAYER

*Loving God, in the words of Dag Hammarskjöld: 'For all that has been, thanks. For all that shall be, yes!'**Amen*

---

* Joseph Hart (1712–64).

** Dag Hammarskjöld (1905–61), from *Markings* (Random House, 2006).

Psalm 23:6b; John 10:27–28 (NIV 1984)

Security

I will dwell in the house of the Lord forever.

[Jesus said,] 'My sheep listen to my voice; I know them, and they follow me. I give them eternal life, and they shall never perish; no-one can snatch them out of my hand.'

Do your thoughts ever turn towards heaven? I guess that many of us, as we get older, instinctively begin to think more about our heavenly future. Here, we are given great assurance that, with Jesus as our shepherd, we have nothing to fear. Dying will simply be going home to the house of the Lord, the mansion that Jesus spoke about with its many rooms (John 14:2).

I know that some believers, in their later years, are plagued by terrible doubts. Some fear that their lives have been wasted and their work in vain; others wonder about their salvation and if they are really saved. Such dark thoughts are simply part of the depression that often encircles us as we confront our mortality, but are also I think part of Satan's attempt to rob us of our joy and peace.

If we find ourselves assailed in this way, we can take courage from the promise of the good shepherd that he has given us eternal life and nothing can change that. No one can snatch us from his hand. We are safe and secure. Nothing we have done will have been wasted. In the Lord, our labour is never in vain.

■ PRAYER

Loving God, thank you for your promise of eternal life. Please take my hand when I doubt or stumble. Amen

Food for thought

Sue Richards

Our church holds a monthly meeting for the older folk of the town, where the gospel is shared alongside friendship, singing and a scrumptious tea. It's called Food for Thought, which is a neat way to encompass two things which are close to many of our hearts – eating and worshipping. The writer of Ecclesiastes puts it well:

> I know that there is nothing better for people than to be happy and to do good while they live. That each of them may eat and drink, and find satisfaction in all their toil – this is the gift of God.
> ECCLESIASTES 3:12–13 (NIV)

There are many references in the Bible to food. We're encouraged to nourish our bodies and souls with both physical and spiritual food, and food also plays an important part in sharing, celebrating and building relationships.

We're going to look at some of those verses in the coming days and remind ourselves of God's amazing provision for our physical and spiritual health.

As the psalmist says:

> He makes grass grow for the cattle,
>   and plants for people to cultivate –
>   bringing forth food from the earth:
> wine that gladdens human hearts,
>   oil to make their faces shine,
>   and bread that sustains their hearts.
> PSALM 104:14–15 (NIV)

Proverbs 22:9 (NIV 1984)

Twice blessed

A generous man will himself be blessed, for he shares his food with the poor.

For the last five years, I've really enjoyed being part of the breakfast team for the night shelter which our church hosts weekly during the winter months. It's a pleasure to provide for our guests, who are always ready and waiting for their plates of full English before they go off into the cold and often empty day. I never know exactly how many we'll be catering for when I go shopping, but there is always plenty of food, with enough to make up sandwiches for people to take away with them and enough for the team too.

When we serve our guests, we know that we are also serving our Lord, as Matthew 25:35 says: 'For I was hungry and you gave me something to eat, I was thirsty and you gave me something to drink.'

Our prayer is that they will take something more than just the extra food and the clean socks with them when they go: a sense of being respected and valued and having moved closer to an encounter with God.

It is always heart-warming to provide for others in this way and, although our motivation is to show God's love and compassion, we know that we too benefit from that blessing.

■ **PRAYER**

Lord, thank you for giving so much to us. Help us to give to others in return. Amen

Deuteronomy 8:3 (ESV)

Spiritual food

And he humbled you and let you hunger and fed you with manna, which you did not know, nor did your fathers know, that he might make you know that man does not live by bread alone, but man lives by every word that comes from the mouth of the Lord.

Several years ago, when my husband and I were on holiday, we visited a church one Sunday and were made to feel very welcome. It was a Communion service and there was a large congregation, so there were several servers, each with a plate and cup. The remains of the bread were placed on the lower tier of a trolley, which was positioned near the exit.

At the end of the service, we prepared to leave and my husband harnessed up his guide dog, Ross. As we passed the trolley, Ross swiped an entire roll without breaking his stride. Thankfully, everyone saw the funny side, but I often picture the incident when I think of 'spiritual food'.

We know that nourishing food and drink are essential for our physical health, and we wouldn't willingly go for long without eating and drinking. But we can forget that we also need to feed our souls regularly, with prayer, teaching, fellowship and service. We should be thirsting and hungering to know Jesus better. Even if we can't attend services, we might still listen to worship music, audio books and services on the radio, read the Bible and Christian books and, above all, spend time in prayer. To stay healthy spiritually, we need to be fed.

■ PRAYER

Heavenly Lord, thank you for providing me with food for my body and food for my soul. Amen

Psalm 107:8–9 (NIV)

God provides

Let them give thanks to the Lord for his unfailing love and his wonderful deeds for mankind, for he satisfies the thirsty and fills the hungry with good things.

I expect your church or supermarket, like mine, has a box where people can donate items to the local food bank when they do their weekly shop. Initially, there were several packets of pasta and rice and perhaps not enough long-life milk or tea bags, but the food bank now issues a list from time to time to let people know what they need most urgently and also some of the more unexpected items that they sometimes welcome.

Once I'd decided what I would give and got into the habit of adding it to my weekly shopping list, it was an easy way to support such a good cause, and I'm glad to have the opportunity to do so.

Over the years, God has met so many of my needs – sometimes with an abundance and generosity that I could hardly believe. To be able to help others with the basic necessities of life seems to be exactly what we're called to do in these lines from Psalm 107. We can all at least play a part in ensuring that the people who live in our locality are not left hungry and thirsty.

■ **PRAYER**

Heavenly Father, thank you for meeting my needs in so many ways. Help me always to be aware of how I can help to meet the needs of others. Amen

Luke 15:23–24 (NIV)

Celebrate

'Bring the fattened calf and kill it. Let's have a feast and celebrate. For this son of mine was dead and is alive again; he was lost and is found.' So they began to celebrate.

Like most families, mine likes to get together for a meal to celebrate special occasions. I come from a family of four daughters, so with a couple of visiting grandparents, assorted boyfriends and one or two waifs and strays, there were frequently ten or more of us sitting around the table. I have many happy memories of those days and rejoice in the hospitable nature of my parents, who made everyone welcome at the family feast.

There are many examples in the Bible of people eating together in fellowship and celebration, and as Christians we continue this tradition, in simple gatherings from week to week and on high days and holy days.

The heart of our celebrations is the love we share in Christ and the knowledge that every good thing we have comes from him. Any meal served with love can become a feast, whether we're eating the simplest of fare or the grandest of meals. As we eat and drink, we can rejoice that we have a God who wants to share in all our celebrations and is there in our midst, delighting in our joy.

■ PRAYER

Thank you, Father, that you are with us in all our celebrations. Help us to delight in your generosity and presence, as you delight in our joy. Amen

Acts 13:2–3 (NIV)

Fasting not feasting

While they were worshipping the Lord and fasting, the Holy Spirit said, 'Set apart for me Barnabas and Saul for the work to which I have called them.' So after they had fasted and prayed, they placed their hands on them and sent them off.

During my first term at college, I took part in a 24-hour fast to raise funds for and awareness of a homeless charity. We camped in a church hall on Friday night and spent Saturday on the streets making cardboard shelters, holding collection boxes and giving out leaflets. I vividly remember dashing back to the dining hall that evening, having never felt so hungry. I'm not sure how much we raised, but the whole experience had quite an impact on me, as I realised that life was really like that for many people.

Fasting isn't a specifically Christian tradition – some other religions are commanded to do it, which we are not – but there is a biblical pattern of fasting at key moments in the early church. Jesus gave instructions for 'when you fast' (Matthew 6:16), not 'if'.

Depending on our health and circumstances, perhaps we might consider how we could fast from time to time, as a way of expressing our longing for God and discerning his will, as well as identifying with those who will go to bed hungry.

■ **PRAYER**

Lord, please show me if this is something you wish me to do as a way of drawing closer to you. Amen

Nehemiah 8:10–11 (ESV)

Sharing is caring

Then [Nehemiah] said to them, 'Go on your way. Eat the fat and drink sweet wine and send portions to anyone who has nothing ready, for this day is holy to our Lord. And do not be grieved, for the joy of the Lord is your strength.' So the Levites calmed all the people, saying, 'Be quiet, for this day is holy; do not be grieved.'

Our monthly Torch Fellowship meeting for visually impaired people is always well attended, and we know that our guests appreciate the lifts, the welcome, the worship and the message. But sometimes the most significant moments occur when we're seated around the tables eating a delicious tea. Somehow, the opportunity to talk to someone over sandwiches and cake opens up conversations and enables people to draw closer together, share fears and support one another.

Although there's lots of busyness as we pour tea, clear plates, wash up and put away tables, the most important thing we can do is to sit alongside someone who is perhaps losing their sight or has concerns about their family, and just listen and offer to pray.

Perhaps there are people in your church, neighbourhood or care home who would appreciate an invitation to share a simple meal or a cup of tea with you and so deepen relationships over food and drink.

■ PRAYER

Lord, show me who you would like me to invite for a cup of tea or a meal. Help me to develop that gift of hospitality, and the listening and prayer that go with it. Amen

Proverbs 15:15–17 (NIV)

Peace rather than plenty

All the days of the oppressed are wretched, but the cheerful heart has a continual feast. Better a little with the fear of the Lord than great wealth with turmoil. Better a dish of vegetables with love than a fattened calf with hatred.

My husband, son and I visited Fran, a blind Christian, in Albania several years ago. We stayed with his pastor, as Fran's family had no room to accommodate us and were concerned about my husband coping with the hole-in-the-ground loo in a hut at the end of the garden.

We were there for a meal one day, but we'd unexpectedly been invited somewhere else beforehand and had food heaped upon us. We were already full, but it was made very clear that we mustn't let Fran's wife know that we'd eaten. Imagine our horror when we saw his son wringing the neck of one of their two chickens to serve to us as honoured guests. Of course, we couldn't not eat the meal. We made a brave attempt, but we didn't do justice to our hosts' generosity.

Whether we're rich or poor, whatever resources we have, whether they are many or few, God calls us to give with generous hearts. But whatever is on the table – a dish of vegetables or the choicest meats – we can meet together in peace and unity when Jesus is at the centre.

■ **PRAYER**
Heavenly Father, please provide for your people throughout the world, and help me to share what I have with a generous spirit. Amen

1 Kings 19:7–8 (NIV)

Sustenance

The angel of the Lord came back a second time and touched [Elijah] and said, 'Get up and eat, for the journey is too much for you.' So he got up and ate and drank. Strengthened by that food, he travelled for forty days and forty nights until he reached Horeb, the mountain of God.

For several years now, I have been a coeliac – intolerant to gluten – which can be a real pain. But 30 years ago, I had to order my bread, several loaves at a time, from the chemist, and if I ran out before the next delivery – tough. It's very different nowadays, with lots of good-quality gluten-free foods available in every supermarket.

We all need a variety of food to sustain us, and God has provided a cornucopia for our nourishment. He knows what we need before we ask.

As Elijah was sustained in the wilderness for 40 days and nights, we too need to eat those foods which will give us physical strength and keep us well. Most of us have plenty of healthy food in the cupboard, and a few treats too, but there are millions across the world who have to survive on the most meagre of portions and on foods with little nutritional value. Unjust economic systems, war and climate change can prevent people getting the nourishment they need, despite God's provision.

■ PRAYER

Loving Lord, show us how we can help to provide for our brothers and sisters who are without enough to eat. Amen

Malachi 3:10 (NIV, abridged)

The bounty of God

'Bring the whole tithe into the storehouse, that there may be food in my house…' says the Lord Almighty, 'and see if I will not throw open the floodgates of heaven and pour out so much blessing that there will not be room enough to store it.'

Whenever we have a bring-and-share meal at church, there is always an amazing variety of food. There is plenty for everyone, including those who don't bring anything, and if you have a portion of chilli on the same plate as a cheese sandwich and some samosas, then so much the better!

It's never formally planned, and we never know how many will turn up, but without fail there is enough and more to spare. Like the story of Jesus feeding 5,000 people with a few loaves and fishes, it's another example of the glorious bounty of God.

As Isaiah 25:6 says, 'The Lord Almighty will prepare a feast of rich food for all peoples, a banquet of aged wine – the best of meats and the finest of wines.'

God not only provides for our physical needs, but he also gives us an abundance of good things to satisfy our spiritual needs: forgiveness, grace, mercy and peace. And just as we are called to share our food with others, so we are called to share God's spiritual gifts with those who don't yet know his love.

■ PRAYER

Bountiful God, help me to share your riches and blessings as widely and generously as I can, in your strength. Amen

1 Timothy 6:6–8 (NIV)

Being content

But godliness with contentment is great gain. For we brought nothing into the world, and we cannot take anything out of it. But if we have food and clothing, we will be content with that.

When I was a child, my mum often said a prayer when she returned from the supermarket, laden down with bags to feed her growing family. She used to say, 'Thank you, Lord, that I have a family to provide for, the money to buy what we need and a car to get it all home.' The words of that prayer have always stayed with me.

It seemed a bit twee at the time, but as an adult I have become so much more aware of the millions of people who would love to make that their prayer, but can't.

It can be so easy to take what we have for granted, instead of acknowledging that God is the source of everything we have and being content with whatever that may be.

Sometimes we may have gifts only for a season, and we can lose the things we once enjoyed. But if we can learn to be grateful to God in all our circumstances, that is a powerful witness in a world driven by the craving for more.

■ **PRAYER**

Gracious Lord, thank you for all your provision to me. Grant me an ever-grateful heart. Amen

The Gift of Years

Debbie Thrower is the pioneer of BRF's Anna Chaplaincy for Older People ministry, offering spiritual care to older people, and is widely involved in training and advocacy.

Visit **annachaplaincy.org.uk** to find out more.

Debbie writes...

Welcome! If it's true that 'you are what you eat', then might it be equally true that 'you are what you read'? These Bible reflections are designed to feed the soul and the imagination. By reading the thoughts of others on this path of ageing, I hope we each find food and light for the journey within these pages.

Paul urged Timothy 'to rekindle the gift of God that is within you... for God did not give us a spirit of cowardice, but rather a spirit of power and of love and of self-discipline' (2 Timothy 1:6–7, NRSV).

Reading these Bible reflections is an encouragement on life's somewhat steeper path in older age, and a form of self-discipline as we commit time to faithfully reading God's word – 'to mark, learn and inwardly digest it', as that lovely Prayer Book collect for the second Sunday of Advent expresses it.

Paul believed that what you fill your mind with really matters: 'Finally, brothers and sisters, whatever is true, whatever is noble, whatever is right, whatever is pure, whatever is lovely, whatever is admirable – if anything is excellent or praiseworthy – think about such things... and the God of peace will be with you' (Philippians 4:8–9, NIV).

In which case... bon appétit!

My best wishes

Debbie

Meet the writer: 'Tricia Williams

'Tricia Williams is the creator and original editor of *Bible Reflections for Older People* and reluctantly gave up the role in order to complete her doctoral thesis on faith and dementia. Originally a teacher, 'Tricia has had a long career as a writer and editor, specialising in Bible resources. She is married to fellow writer Emlyn and they have two adult children and a shared love of France. She was brought up in a small village in the New Forest. She says:

'My lovely mum and dad were very committed Christians, and life centred around our little Baptist chapel. This was a thatched chapel which was built by my ancestors in the middle of the 19th century. So I had a very lively, loving, small-community upbringing centred around Christian activity, and I'm thankful to my parents for that and for the love of the Bible and the focus on serving God as our direction of life.'

But was there a point when faith became more personal to her – a transition between what she'd inherited and it becoming her own?

'Yes. In one sense God was always there. God was the head of the household, and life was about pleasing God in the way we were living. But around the age of 12 or 13, I began to realise that this had something to do with me personally, and I did need to make a choice to be a follower of Jesus. So there was a progression as I grew into that personal desire to serve him, and that continued as I went on through my teens, thinking, "Okay, so what does this mean for my life?"'

'Tricia completed a General Arts degree and then went on to study for her PGCE at Exeter University, where, she says, 'I had a wonderful year and I thought a lot about education, faith and young people.

'That wasn't necessarily the intention of the lecturers, but lots of their questions about the meaning of human life and the meaning of education helped me begin to think deeply about how, as a Christian, I wanted to help young people grow.'

After five years teaching English in secondary school, she moved to a role in the Schools Ministry team at Scripture Union, speaking, writing, training and pastoring young Christians in schools.

'That led to more writing,' she explains. 'I wrote a book about being a Christian at school and lots of Bible resources. Because of my Christian background, I had a good knowledge of scripture and a real interest in making that accessible to other people. I saw Bible resources as a major way of helping people to come into relationship with God and grow in their faith.'

She and Emlyn met at Scripture Union, settled for a while in Cambridge and then moved to Australia.

'Emlyn worked in schools with Scripture Union, and I spent quite a lot of my time focused on having babies – I have two Australian-born children. I did some editorial training and freelance editing alongside caring for the children and was asked more and more to do bits of writing.'

They returned to the UK in 1991 and 'Tricia became a commissioning editor with Scripture Union.

'At first my interest was in 11–14-year-olds, because that was my children's age group, but as they got older and left home, my work at Scripture Union developed and my focus shifted to adult Bible notes, including *Daily Bread*, *Encounter with God* and *Closer to God*. Also around that time, I began to be interested in contextual theology – how do people in different situations understand the Bible? How do they engage with scripture and grow in their relationship with God?

'So I did a master's degree in contextual and practical theology. Then, as time went on, I became more involved in thinking about older people because I was getting older myself, and my relatives and friends were getting older, so I began to think about what this meant in terms of faith.

'I got to know people who had dementia and realised that they were people who had been involved in leadership, in teaching and in preaching – and now they have dementia. So how does that affect their relationship with God? What is the nature of faith in God when your cognitive ability is compromised by dementia? That triggered my interest in faith and dementia, and eventually I began to work on my doctoral thesis with Professor John Swinton at Aberdeen University.'

Doctorates are notoriously demanding on many different levels. What sustained 'Tricia through five gruelling years of research and writing?

'I guess what got me through was a sense of calling – just feeling, to begin with, that no one else was doing that particular piece of work. Then, also, my empirical research was very moving. People trusted me incredibly to talk to me, and their families did as well, in allowing me to be with them, recording them. And all those glimpses of deep, deep faith – they helped me to keep going.

'What else got me through? Grit, determination – and a very loving husband whom I talked to endlessly. I know I had people praying for me, believing that this was a worthwhile project, and I felt I had a real responsibility to the families I'd spoken to, who had trusted me so profoundly.'

To find out more about 'Tricia's research findings, see her blog post for 'Faith in Later Life':
faithinlaterlife.org/news-blog-what-happens-to-faith-when-christians-get-dementia

The Flower

George Herbert (3 April 1593–1 March 1633) is one of the best loved in a long line of Anglican poet-priests. Modest and retiring, he spent his last years as Rector of Bemerton near Salisbury. Here in 'The Flower', Herbert links the return of greenness and new life in nature with renewed faith in God.

The Flower

How fresh, oh Lord, how sweet and clean
Are thy returns! even as the flowers in spring;
To which, besides their own demean,
The late-past frosts tributes of pleasure bring.
Grief melts away
Like snow in May,
As if there were no such cold thing.

Who would have thought my shrivelled heart
Could have recovered greenness? It was gone
Quite underground; as flowers depart
To see their mother-root, when they have blown,
Where they together
All the hard weather,
Dead to the world, keep house unknown.

These are thy wonders, Lord of power,
Killing and quickening, bringing down to hell
And up to heaven in an hour;
Making a chiming of a passing-bell.
We say amiss
This or that is:
Thy word is all, if we could spell.

Oh that I once past changing were,
Fast in thy Paradise, where no flower can wither!
Many a spring I shoot up fair,
Offering at heaven, growing and groaning thither;
Nor doth my flower
Want a spring shower,
My sins and I joining together.

But while I grow in a straight line,
Still upwards bent, as if heaven were mine own,
Thy anger comes, and I decline:
What frost to that? what pole is not the zone
Where all things burn,
When thou dost turn,
And the least frown of thine is shown?

And now in age I bud again,
After so many deaths I live and write;
I once more smell the dew and rain,
And relish versing. Oh, my only light,
It cannot be
That I am he
On whom thy tempests fell all night.

These are thy wonders, Lord of love,
To make us see we are but flowers that glide;
Which when we once can find and prove,
Thou hast a garden for us where to bide;
Who would be more,
Swelling through store,
Forfeit their Paradise by their pride.

George Herbert (1593–1633)

Meet Angela Lucas

Life begins at 60! **Angela Lucas**, now 86, has five adult children and eleven grandchildren, and has spent the last 25 years challenging herself to do new things. She writes:

It all began when I enrolled at our local college to study for an A Level in English Literature when I was 60. At the end of the course, the young students were filling in their university applications, and it suddenly occurred to me that I could do the same.

I collected a form from a rather bemused secretary and spent the next three years studying Humanities at Anglia Ruskin University. It was challenging, but by the end I was hooked on studying and did a course in Pastoral Theology with the Cambridge Theological Federation and then a creative writing degree with the Open University. This was a rather different experience and required a lot of self-discipline.

My work life has been in nursing. I worked in the Queen Alexandra's Army Nursing Corps for six years and then in various nursing jobs before becoming a medical secretary, first for our local hospice and then in Saudi Arabia for a year. Alongside all this I was a Marie Curie nurse for 25 years. Then in my 60s I went to Egypt to teach English at the British Council using TEFL and studied Arabic.

My faith in Jesus is a core value and a continual steep learning curve. I have made many wrong and foolish decisions, but I know God's love for me isn't dependent on any form of goodness, but rather on the endless grace of God. Knowing his forgiveness has enabled me to pick myself up, dust myself down and move forward.

On my 82nd birthday, I was challenged to walk the last 100 miles of the ancient pilgrim route El Camino de Santiago, in northern Spain, and then I wrote a book (*How to be a SuperAger*, Panoma Press, 2018) to inspire other people who are perhaps struggling with the ageing process.

It was published last year, just three weeks before my home was destroyed by a fire which spread from next door. I was given accommodation in our local Premier Inn and then was able to rent a small house next door but one, until my rebuilt home was handed back to me one year later.

During that year I was diagnosed with early-stage breast cancer, so it was a challenging time, but I chose to focus on the words 'early stage'.

I don't think of myself as particularly adventurous and outgoing – it seems rather that I simply fell into opportunities – but I have had too many friends die far too soon, so I feel it would be disrespectful to waste my life.

I felt that once my children had left home, the choice was mine as to whether I simply withered away or blossomed in a new stage of life. My advice to others is to keep breathing, dust yourself down when the going gets tough and make the most of the challenges and opportunities life brings.

This article was first published in *Woman Alive* magazine, September 2019, and is reprinted with kind permission.

Jesus and animals

Roger Combes

A horse and its rider, a shepherd and his dog, a much-loved pet and its owner – all show just how close a relationship between animals and humans can be. Animals are an important part of God's creation and of our lives. We rarely go anywhere without seeing or hearing them, and it would be a bleak, impossible world without them. In many parts of the globe, human life depends heavily on working animals.

Animals and birds were a part of Jesus' life, as they are part of ours, and he often talked about them. Sheep are mentioned 40 times in the gospels, birds 30 times and fish 30 times; also dogs, 'wild animals', camels, oxen, snakes, donkeys, wolves, foxes, goats and pigs. One author describes Jesus as 'a man familiar with the world of nature. He is observant, knowledgeable, compassionate.'*

As we shall see, Jesus frequently referred to animals in order to make a point or to illustrate what he was saying. He was clear that God provides and cares for animals, and so should we.

* Tony Sargent, *Animal Rights and Wrongs: A biblical perspective* (Hodder & Stoughton, 1996), p. 95.

Luke 13:34; 19:41 (NIV)

A hen and her chicks

'Jerusalem, Jerusalem, you who kill the prophets and stone those sent to you, how often I have longed to gather your children together as a hen gathers her chicks under her wings, and you were not willing...' As [Jesus] approached Jerusalem and saw the city, he wept over it.

There were strange noises coming from the kitchen, so I went to have a look. Inside, bizarrely, a pigeon was flying around, trying to escape. But as I approached, it panicked all the more and resisted my clumsy efforts to catch it and set it free. I found myself talking to it: 'Come on, don't be frightened. I'm trying to help you. I'm on your side.' But I don't think it believed me.

Jesus had the same problem with Jerusalem. His own people 'knew him not' and resisted him as he tried to help them. He said he felt like a mother hen trying to shelter her chicks from danger and yet they refused.

Jesus must surely have seen a hen instinctively spreading wide her wings to protect her brood. Our Lord Jesus is merciful and kind by nature. He is always drawing us to himself, to save us from ourselves and to help us. Why, as one hymn puts it, would we scatter from a love so true and deep?

■ **PRAYER**

Hide me, O my Saviour, hide,
till the storm of life is past...
Cover my defenceless head
*with the shadow of thy wing.**
Amen

* Charles Wesley, 'Jesus, lover of my soul'.

Luke 15:4–7 (NIV, abridged)

Finding a lost sheep

'Suppose one of you has a hundred sheep and loses one of them… When he finds it… he calls his friends and neighbours together and says, "Rejoice with me; I have found my lost sheep." I tell you that in the same way there will be more rejoicing in heaven over one sinner who repents than over ninety-nine righteous people who do not need to repent.'

We were having a coffee in the airport, waiting for our flight to be called, when one of our party could not find her passport. Keeping rising anxiety under control, we asked at the airline desk what to do. They told us that the passport had been handed in and we could pick it up at the departure gate. Big relief all round.

Jesus tells of a shepherd finding his one lost sheep. We can easily imagine the shepherd's relief, yomping over the hills with a smile on his face and the exhausted animal on his shoulders. Soon, the whole village is celebrating with him.

Heaven's best parties are held when someone repents. Jesus intended his hearers, and us, always to rejoice when someone turns to him, however despised, lost or sinful they may have been before. Heaven's way is always to welcome each one with joy.

Turning from wrong ourselves will bring new joy to God and his angels. This is a great incentive to repent. Make heaven happy today.

■ PRAYER

Merciful Father, may those turning to Christ today from different kinds of lostness find a welcome and help from your people. Amen

Matthew 10:29–31; Luke 12:24 (NIV, abridged)

Sparrows and ravens

'Are not two sparrows sold for a penny? Yet not one of them will fall to the ground outside your Father's care... So don't be afraid; you are worth more than many sparrows.'

'Consider the ravens. They do not sow or reap, they have no store-room or barn; yet God feeds them. And how much more valuable are you than birds!'

When I was a boy, I remember our small garden lawn being covered by masses of sparrows, and I have always liked these busy, cheerful little creatures. Jesus says that one of them cannot so much as fall without our heavenly Father knowing about it and caring.

Ravens are bigger and more aggressive birds. A famous tourist attraction at the Tower of London, they are graceful in the air and intelligent. They are also confident scavengers, helping to keep the countryside clean. Wonderfully, God cares for them too. 'God feeds them,' says Jesus.

If God cares for birds, then we ought to also. But Jesus' main point here is that we should not be fearful. We matter to our heavenly Father and he cares for us. We may be vulnerable, as birds are, and our lives may be precarious, like theirs. But fear not. Our Father in heaven, who values the sparrows and ravens, values us much, much more.

■ PRAYER

Heavenly Father, thank you that nothing happens in my life that you don't know about, and thank you that you care for me and support me in all my ups and downs, through Jesus Christ. Amen

John 10:3, 11, 14, 27–28 (NIV, abridged)

My sheep

'[The shepherd] calls his own sheep by name and leads them out… The good shepherd lays down his life for the sheep… I am the good shepherd; I know my sheep and my sheep know me… My sheep listen to my voice… and they follow me. I give them eternal life, and they shall never perish; no one will snatch them out of my hand.'

Does your dog or your cat know that it belongs to you? 'Of course,' says the owner. Many animals seem to have some sense of whom they belong to. Even wild chimpanzees in a protected tropical forest recognise their rangers. In Bible times, a shepherd did not have a dog to help him; instead, he relied on knowing his sheep and on the sheep's sense of knowing the shepherd. In some rudimentary way, they seemed to know which was their shepherd. So they followed him when he called.

'My' is a key word here. Jesus refers to his followers as '*my* sheep', just as we say, 'The Lord is *my* shepherd.' This mutual belonging is personal. He knows us by our name and he knows us completely. His words resonate with us and they are compelling. This belonging is eternal life. It is indestructible. No one shall snatch us out of his hand – ever.

■ PRAYER

Thank you, Lord Jesus, that you are still the good shepherd, and that I belong to you and you belong to me. Amen

Luke 18:25, 27; Matthew 23:23–24 (NIV, abridged)

Two camel sayings

'It is easier for a camel to go through the eye of a needle than for someone who is rich to enter the kingdom of heaven... What is impossible with man is possible with God.'

'You hypocrites! You give a tenth of your spices... But you have neglected the more important matters of the law – justice, mercy and faithfulness... You strain out a gnat but swallow a camel.'

Have you ever sat on a camel while it was getting to its feet? It's an awkward, even comical, experience. But camels have been vital for desert travellers for thousands of years, and Jesus twice refers to these remarkable creatures in his teaching. Each time he uses their ungainly size to illustrate the absurd.

Some of us find it hard to get a thread of cotton through a needle to sew on a button. But threading a camel through a needle – that's ridiculous. It is humanly impossible. Then comes the good news: God does the impossible. The most unlikely people – anyone, in fact – can enter the kingdom of heaven. It's God's best miracle.

In a separate saying, Jesus could be describing a fastidious tea-drinker who strains out every tiny tea leaf, but then swallows a camel. Absurd – just as people who insist on some minor point of their religion but (sw)allow injustice, lies and cruelty are absurd. Jesus calls them hypocrites.

■ **PRAYER**

Jesus, may my priorities always be important things that really matter to you. Amen

Matthew 7:15; 10:16 (NIV)

Wolves, snakes and doves

'Watch out for false prophets. They come to you in sheep's clothing, but inwardly they are ferocious wolves... I am sending you out like sheep among wolves. Therefore be as shrewd as snakes and as innocent as doves.'

The voice on the phone sounds so genuine. But it's not. It is a fraud. It says, 'There is a fault on your computer.' There is not. 'This is your bank protecting your account.' It is not. Or, 'Invest in our profit-generating investment.' Investment disaster, more likely. We need to be on our guard.

Jesus warned against wolves 'in sheep's clothing'. They look harmless, but they are out to devour us or our money. We might call them 'sharks' today. Even in religious contexts, we can be deceived by those who pose as true but are false. Watch out for them, Jesus said.

On a different occasion, when he was sending his disciples out into the world, Jesus recognised that they were vulnerable, like sheep being sent into a pack of wolves – just as he himself was. He urged the disciples to be as wise as serpents and as innocent as doves, and he says the same to us in our world today. We need to keep our wits about us and to be honest and true at all times.

■ PRAYER

Lord Jesus, you were a faithful witness in our world. May your Holy Spirit give us discernment to know what is true and good, and the wisdom to act on it faithfully. Amen

Luke 9:57–58 (NIV)

Foxes have holes

As they were walking along the road, a man said to him, 'I will follow you wherever you go.' Jesus replied, 'Foxes have dens and birds have nests, but the Son of Man has nowhere to lay his head.'

As an observant country-dweller, Jesus must have caught sight of many a fox slinking off home after a night's work. That's the point. The free-ranging fox had a home to go to; Jesus didn't.

In today's world, it is not unusual to have to work away from home for months on end, and it is hard. In later years, we sometimes need to leave a long-established home to be nearer family or for other reasons. When Jesus left his home to begin his ministry, it might well have been a painful step. He understands how it feels. He knows what hearth and home mean to us.

In 1944, Betsie ten Boom, a devout Dutch woman, aged 59, was sent to Ravensbrück concentration camp, where she died, for sheltering Jewish fugitives in her home. Soon after her arrest, as she was stripped of her clothes and belongings, she suddenly remembered that Jesus had been stripped when he was arrested. She was humbled and proud to be following him. Jesus urges his disciples to keep on following him, even if we miss some of our creature comforts.

■ PRAYER

Pray for Christian men and women and families who have left their homes to serve Christ in another country or culture.

Luke 13:15b; 14:5 (NIV)

Ox-in-pit drama

'Doesn't each of you on the Sabbath untie your ox or donkey from the stall and lead it out to give it water?… If one of you has a child or an ox that falls into a well on the Sabbath day, will you not immediately pull it out?'

What do you do if an emergency occurs at a weekend? You act immediately if you can to fix it, at least for the time being. Jesus' discussion with his hearers took much the same line. He knew that his listeners would water their animals, even on the sabbath, and rush to save them in an emergency, even on the sabbath. Jesus clearly approved.

Donkeys and oxen played a big part in family and community life. A donkey was essential for travel and transporting things, rather like a car or small van today. An ox was like a tractor, used for heavy farming work. A wise owner and his family would value their working animals and understand them. Caring for them would be a priority every day.

Jesus the healer was insisting that the well-being of people was at least as important as the welfare of their animals. In fact, the two go together in Jesus' thinking: people and animals both need care and compassion.

■ **PRAYER**

Pray for all animal-owners, farmers, vets and rangers. May our world be a place where adults and children learn to respect and protect the animal world.

Mark 11:1b–3 (NIV)

On a donkey

Jesus sent two of his disciples, saying to them, 'Go to the village ahead of you, and just as you enter it, you will find a colt tied there, which no one has ever ridden. Untie it and bring it here. If anyone asks you, "Why are you doing this?" say, "The Lord needs it and will send it back here shortly."'

A bucking bronco at a cowboy rodeo usually throws its rider within seconds. Breaking in a horse takes time and patience. By contrast, when Jesus borrows a colt that has never had anyone on its back, it carries him into Jerusalem through noisy crowds calmly and without fuss.

This is the only occasion we read of Jesus riding on a donkey. Usually he walked with his disciples. So why did he say he needed a donkey now? He needed it for a piece of drama to show people who he was, in the words of the prophet Zechariah (9:9): 'Your king comes to you, righteous and victorious, lowly and riding on a donkey, on a colt, the foal of a donkey.' The crowds knew their scripture, got the point and rejoiced.

It might be surprising that the Lord of glory should need the services of a humble donkey – and surprising, but true, that he needs us to serve him. May our response be as willing and faithful as the donkey's.

■ PRAYER

Lord, I feel a bit of a donkey sometimes, but may I carry you into the city, town or village where I live. Amen

Matthew 25:31–32 (NIV)

Sheep and goats

'When the Son of Man comes in his glory, and all the angels with him, he will sit on his glorious throne. All the nations will be gathered before him, and he will separate the people one from another as a shepherd separates the sheep from the goats.'

'Chalk and cheese' is what we sometimes say about complete opposites. Brothers or sisters may look alike but have quite different personalities: one may be sporty and outgoing, and the other artistic and self-effacing.

'Sheep and goats' was Jesus' phrase when describing how he will differentiate between the people in front of him. They may appear indistinguishable, but he will separate them like a shepherd sorting sheep from goats.

And one of the things that will help him decide is if people have helped those in need. In the mind of the Son of Man, there is a big divide between those who help the hungry, the sick, the oppressed and the imprisoned – and those who don't. Sheep and goats.

Jesus notices if someone helps you when you are in need. And he notices if you help his brothers and sisters when they are in need. It really matters to him.

■ **PRAYER**

Pray for Christian Aid, Tearfund and similar agencies seeking to bring practical aid in Christ's name to those in great need.

Keeping faith

'Tricia Williams

Long years of experiencing God's faithfulness may bring us an enduring, underlying sense of peace, which younger people may struggle to find. Even so, perhaps we sometimes feel overwhelmed by the times in which we live.

So how should we, as older people of faith, respond to disturbing aspects of our world? What can we – who can feel relatively powerless – do in the face of crises and suffering?

Not surprisingly, the Bible speaks of a world in which there will always be troubles. Yet however it might sometimes appear, it is a world in which a sovereign, just and loving God is at work. And, of course, Jesus' own suffering reminds us that he loves this world and that he identifies with and understands the deepest pain human beings can ever experience.

It can be easy to feel overwhelmed by the troubles we see – and to assume that we can do nothing. But God's word points to a different response. The lives of faithful individuals – even 'little old me' (author speaking) – do matter and do make a difference.

As you come to read God's word and pray, take a moment to remember the apostle Peter's words: 'Cast all your anxiety on him because he cares for you' (1 Peter 5:7, NIV).

Psalm 97:1–2, 9–10 (NIV, abridged)

Our God reigns!

The Lord reigns, let the earth be glad… Righteousness and justice are the foundation of his throne… For you, Lord, are the Most High over all the earth; you are far above all gods. Let those who love the Lord hate evil, for he guards the lives of his faithful ones.

'Who's in charge here?' Gwen demanded crossly, in a moment of too much busyness in the care home where she was living. In a confusing situation, she wanted order and to know that someone was in control. Things weren't right. If those feelings echo your own in some way, here's some good news from Psalm 97.

At times, it may seem that no one is in charge in our world. Here, the psalmist gives us three encouraging things to remember.

First, above and beyond the passing rulers of our time, the eternal God, 'the Most High', reigns. He is bigger.

Second, when it no longer seems clear what is right or wrong, God's righteousness and justice are an anchor which helps us stay true in stormy times.

Finally, there is the promise that as we acknowledge him as ruler of our lives and our world, God himself 'guards the lives of his faithful ones'.

We can rest assured: God is in charge. As we seek to live in ways that honour his 'righteousness and justice', he holds us safe in his light and joy.

■ **PRAYER**

Praise God that 'the Lord reigns'! Thank him for his faithfulness to you.

John 16:33 (NIV)

Take heart

'I have told you these things, so that in me you may have peace. In this world you will have trouble. But take heart! I have overcome the world.'

The disciples were confused – 'What does he mean?' they puzzled (16:18). They had hoped that Jesus would be the longed-for Messiah and Saviour of Israel – now he seemed to be speaking of death and defeat (16:16). Their dreams were crashing down. Yet, in spite of this, he speaks of having peace in him and taking heart. How can this be?

They didn't understand that Jesus was no ordinary leader. His coming from God his Father was revolutionary with implications beyond time. The focus of Jesus' words was on his death and resurrection: 'Your grief will turn to joy' (16:20). Evil and pain would be defeated. The peace, or shalom, Jesus speaks of is not a promise of a life without troubles in this world. But it is the whole-person peace of knowing you're right with God whatever happens – and he is right with you: 'the Father himself loves you' (16:27).

In the midst of our troubled world, we can take heart – because Jesus has 'overcome the world'. And as our lives express our own peace and joy in Christ, we can bring others the encouragement of knowing that they too can take heart as they discover God's love for them in Jesus.

■ PRAYER

Lord Jesus, thank you for your peace. Help me to share your love with others today. Amen

Matthew 6:9–10 (NIV)

Seek God's kingdom

'This, then, is how you should pray: "Our Father in heaven, hallowed be your name, your kingdom come, your will be done, on earth as it is in heaven."'

Try to imagine how the world might be different if this prayer were to be answered completely today. What changes might we see in politics and situations where there is war, poverty and hardship, or if everyone really believed that God is our Father? How would lives be changed if we all sought to honour God and his creation as holy – 'hallowed'? What would a world be like where everyone, in every situation, tried to live according to God's good will? Yes, it would be heaven.

Meanwhile, at least until Jesus returns, I don't think 24-hour news reporters are going to be out of a job. This world is a work in progress in which we are called by God to have a part. Jesus' words weren't spoken to people of power, but to humble disciples who were living simple lives day by day. Jesus teaches them to pray that God's kingdom will come in the places where they live: his love, his forgiveness, his generosity, his justice, his rule.

Whatever our own situation, Jesus calls us to join with him in seeking his kingdom and praying that it will come.

■ **PRAYER**

In the small or big events of today, ask God to help you seek his kingdom. 'For thine is the kingdom, and the power, and the glory, forever. Amen' (Matthew 6:13, KJV).

1 Timothy 2:1–2 (NIV)

Pray for leaders

I urge, then, first of all, that petitions, prayers, intercession and thanksgiving be made for all people – for kings and all those in authority, that we may live peaceful and quiet lives in all godliness and holiness.

Can you think of good leaders who have made a difference to your own and others' lives – in our nation, the world, your work, your church, where you live? And what about the opposite? In some countries, people are suffering because leaders are motivated by power and evil. Many Christians across the world live with persecution because of ungodly leadership.

Having power to rule is a life-changing gift from God which needs to be carried with humility and care. The apostle Paul writes elsewhere that such authority is granted by God (Romans 13:1). It is an awesome responsibility. We need to thank God for those who are willing to lead.

Yet, as members of our society, criticising and blaming our leaders can seem to be a national pastime. In these verses, the apostle Paul suggests a different perspective. We should first pray for our leaders: ask God for his intervention in their decisions and thank God for them. And there's a good reason: it's not just the general well-being of society that's at stake, but also the establishment of peaceful freedom which will allow believers to live in ways that serve and honour God, the King of kings.

■ PRAYER

Think of three leaders of whom you are particularly aware. Pray for them today.

Luke 10:27 (NIV)

Keep on loving

'Love the Lord your God with all your heart and with all your soul and with all your strength and with all your mind; and love your neighbour as yourself.'

How should we live in times like these? We're getting older; physically, we're not as active as we once were. What can we do? Jesus' response to the religious teacher takes us back to God's basic guidelines for life – which are for all of us, whatever our situation or age: love God and your neighbour.

This isn't some airy-fairy nice feeling. It's tough and active and involves every part of who we are: heart, soul, strength, mind. It's a determination to put God's way above our own. It overflows into putting our neighbour's well-being first. It may result in surprising decisions which change lives, as well as the 'gentle answer [which] turns away wrath' (Proverbs 15:1).

Jesus tells the story of the good Samaritan to illustrate his point (Luke 10:30–37). Here, the unexpected love of the Samaritan for the injured man involves compassion, time and cost – and it changes the wounded man's life.

Loving God is to be the character of our lives. It is demonstrated in our behaviour and words towards others. Sometimes it will take them by surprise and open their lives to receiving God's own love. Whose life might your loving decisions, words and actions change today?

■ **PRAYER**

Loving God, help me to love others today as you have loved me. Amen

Ephesians 6:18 (NIV)

Keep on praying

And pray in the Spirit on all occasions with all kinds of prayers and requests. With this in mind, be alert and always keep on praying for all the Lord's people.

As a young adult, I once stayed overnight with older Christians whom I didn't know well. In their kitchen, I happened to notice my name on a prayer list pinned to a board. I felt humbled, encouraged and challenged by their unseen service of prayer. No doubt we already pray for others, but how could we develop that practice?

In church, we may hear of prayer needs – illness, difficult decisions, troubling situations. People may also carry serious anxieties but not share them publicly. How alert are we in our understanding and listening, ready to notice and pray?

That word 'always' in today's verse challenges us to pray constantly and imaginatively as we remember others going through their days – living with their struggles. When someone comes to mind, why not pray for them there and then?

This praying 'in the Spirit' gives us the amazing privilege of joining in God's work in our world. The instruction 'keep on' suggests more than a quick one-off prayer. Rather, this is a commitment to prayer which accompanies others, perhaps through long years. If you already have a list of people and situations you pray for every day, why not add a few more names? If you don't have a list, perhaps you could start one now.

■ **PRAYER**

Father God, please be close to _____ [add name/s]. May they know your help and strength today. Amen

Matthew 5:14, 16 (NIV)

Let your light shine

'You are the light of the world... Let your light shine before others, that they may see your good deeds and glorify your Father in heaven.'

It's tempting to retreat from a world that sometimes seems dark – both in the big picture and in the small, everyday interactions we see or hear around us. Our decreasing energy may make us feel that action is for younger people now. Yet Jesus, the light of the world, speaks through scripture to all of his disciples – and that includes us: 'Let your light shine.'

How? This verse makes clear that our behaviour will remind others of our 'Father in heaven'. Just as children reflect the characteristics of their earthly parents, so we are to reflect the light and love of God. It might be as simple as an understanding, welcoming or thankful smile. It will be expressed in the kindness and generosity of the fruit of the Spirit (Galatians 5:22–23). Always, there is purpose – to help others draw closer to God.

Later in the New Testament, the apostle Paul speaks about having this treasure of Christ's light in 'jars of clay' (2 Corinthians 4:7). We may be fragile human beings, but we too can let our light shine. Remember, the tiniest spark of light in a dark room guides others and helps them understand where they are.

■ PRAYER

Remember the old gospel song: 'This little light of mine, I'm gonna let it shine'? Ask God to help you do this today.

Micah 6:8b (NIV)

Walk humbly...

And what does the Lord require of you? To act justly and to love mercy and to walk humbly with your God.

In this big world in which strength, power and wealth are honoured, how should I live for God? The speaker of these words, the prophet Micah, gives a simple solution. Day by day, step by step, his words help us to keep faith with our God.

So, today, how might I live justly, not only in my physical actions, but also in my words and thoughts? At times today, I might feel angry about how others speak to me or act. How can I remember to be merciful and forgive? We are often quick to be insistent or defensive about our own rights and position. How might I walk humbly? How might I serve others today, whether or not anyone else notices?

Being human, these challenges are not simple. Micah's punchline comes at the end of this verse. The power to live like this comes from walking humbly 'with your God', as Jesus showed us by example.

I can't do it on my own. I need to cultivate spending time with God and walking with him through the day – just as we're doing now as we read his word and pray.

■ PRAYER

Just as I am, poor, wretched, blind;
Sight, riches, healing of the mind;
Yes, all I need, in Thee to find,
O Lamb of God, I come, I come!'*
Amen

*Charlotte Elliott (1789–1871).

John 14:27 (NIV)

Receive Christ's peace

'Peace I leave with you; my peace I give you. I do not give to you as the world gives. Do not let your hearts be troubled and do not be afraid.'

Take a moment to remember some of the difficulties in your own life and in the wider world. Now, imagine Jesus standing near you, in the room where you are now. As he sees your troubles, Jesus speaks these words to you. Say them quietly to yourself again.

These words are a gift which Christ offers us. As with all gifts, we need to receive it. I can choose to dwell on, and in, the anxieties life brings. Or I can decide to trust his word and accept his peace. Doing this won't mean that all the world's and my own troubles get solved. This is a different kind of peace, from God himself. As we remembered in an earlier reflection, Jesus encourages us to 'take heart' because he has 'overcome the world' (John 16:33). The problems of time are defeated through Christ for eternity.

We'll still have worries and failures of faith in this life, because we are frail human beings. But with hearts and minds set on Christ – overall, deep within us, holding us close to him – we can know his peace. There is no reason to be troubled or afraid.

■ PRAYER

Jesus said, 'Peace be with you!' and 'Receive the Holy Spirit' (John 20:21–22). Receive Christ's peace now.

Hebrews 12:1–2 (NIV, abridged)

Fix your eyes on Jesus

Therefore, since we are surrounded by such a great cloud of witnesses... let us run with perseverance the race marked out for us, fixing our eyes on Jesus, the pioneer and perfecter of faith. For the joy that was set before him he endured the cross... and sat down at the right hand of the throne of God.

When all else is failing, remember Jesus. When life is a struggle, think of other faithful believers who have gone before (see Hebrews 11). Imagine God's people cheering you on from the stands – and fix your eyes on Jesus.

Why? Because Jesus is the one from God who lived this human life, all the time keeping faith with his Father. He understands our pain, because he endured the anguish of carrying all the suffering of humankind. He has gone ahead. His life, death and resurrection make our faith possible. And at the end of our race, we can look forward with joy to resting with him.

Perseverance has the sense of endurance. This race will need determination, courage and trust as we look ahead to Jesus, 'the pioneer and perfecter of faith'. He is with us in the present and waits for us in the future. Let's keep faith – and keep our eyes on him.

■ PRAYER

Turn your thoughts to Jesus as you say or sing these words:

Turn your eyes upon Jesus.
Look full in his wonderful face.
And the things of earth will grow strangely dim
In the light of his glory and grace.*

* Helen Howarth Lemmel (1863–1961).

Leaving a legacy of faith: the God who endures

When a colleague changes job or retires, or a friend moves on from an area of ministry at church, it can sometimes feel like there is an aching void to fill. I imagine that Elisha may have had much the same feeling as he anticipated Elijah's departure in 2 Kings 2.

His request of Elijah is telling – a double portion of his spirit. The 'double portion' refers to what the eldest son would have expected as his inheritance. As such, Elisha is asking to carry on in Elijah's stead, taking on the responsibilities and opportunities of his ministry.

That his request was granted is shown in the middle of the chapter – Elisha strikes the water with Elijah's cloak, and it parts as it had for Elijah.

Each of us might well ask what we will leave behind – what difference we will have made and what lives we will have changed. In these matters, 2 Kings might encourage us in a couple of directions.

First, we are encouraged to remember that while Elisha had Elijah's cloak, it was God's power that was wielded through it. Our passions and cares are safe in his hands. It is his work; he will see it done.

Second, we're encouraged to find people who share our passions and goals to continue our work and ministry, serving the church and helping individuals of all ages to grow in faith.

If your passions align with ours, would you consider leaving a gift to BRF in your will to allow us to further our ministry? And in all this, please pray that God would work with his mighty power in our midst.

For further information about making a gift to BRF
in your will, please visit **brf.org.uk/lastingdifference**,
contact **+44 (0)1865 319700** or email **giving@brf.org.uk**.

Make the most of
RETIREMENT

Retirement is about new beginnings and new opportunities. In this helpful book, grounded both in personal experience and in extensive research among retired ministers, and rich in quotations from an eclectic range of writers, Paul Beasley-Murray explores how retirement is part of God's rhythm for our lives and provides encouragement and insights for this next stage of the journey. A must-read for lay and ordained Christians alike.

Make the Most of Retirement
Paul Beasley-Murray
978 0 85746 864 2 £7.99
brfonline.org.uk

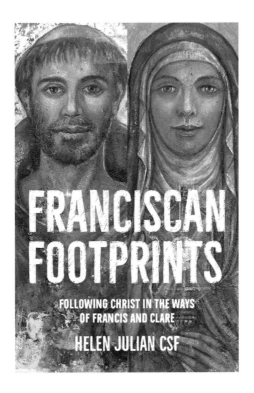

There are many ways of following Christ – each footprint is unique. One of these, the Franciscan spiritual journey, has been tried and tested over the centuries, and the experiences of St Francis and St Clare and all those who have been inspired by their lives still resonate with us. Helen Julian CSF explores the distinctive features of their spirituality and shows how these practices can be applied to, and become part of, our daily lives.

Franciscan Footprints
Following Christ in the ways of Francis and Clare
Helen Julian CSF
978 0 85746 811 6 £8.99
brfonline.org.uk

To order

Online: **brfonline.org.uk**
Telephone: +44 (0)1865 319700
Mon–Fri 9.15–17.30
Post: complete this form and send to the address below

Delivery times within the UK are normally 15 working days. Prices are correct at the time of going to press but may change without prior notice.

Title	Issue*	Price	Qty	Total
Make the Most of Retirement		£7.99		
Franciscan Footprints		£8.99		
Bible Reflections for Older People (single copy)	Sep 20/Jan 21*	£5.15		

delete as appropriate

POSTAGE AND PACKING CHARGES			
Order value	UK	Europe	Rest of world
Under £7.00	£2.00		
£7.00–£29.99	£3.00	Available on request	Available on request
£30.00 and over	FREE		

Total value of books	
Postage and packing	
Total for this order	

Please complete in BLOCK CAPITALS

Title .... First name/initials .... Surname................................

Address ....

.... Postcode ....

Acc. No. .... Telephone ....

Email ....

Method of payment

☐ Cheque (made payable to BRF)   ☐ MasterCard / Visa

Card no. ☐☐☐☐ ☐☐☐☐ ☐☐☐☐ ☐☐☐☐

Expires end ☐☐ ☐☐   Security code* ☐☐☐   Last 3 digits on the reverse of the card

Signature* .... Date .... /............ /............

*ESSENTIAL IN ORDER TO PROCESS YOUR ORDER

Please return this form to:
BRF, 15 The Chambers, Vineyard, Abingdon OX14 3FE | enquiries@brf.org.uk
To read our terms and conditions, please visit **brfonline.org.uk/terms**.

BROP0220

The Bible Reading Fellowship (BRF) is a Registered Charity (233280)

BIBLE REFLECTIONS FOR OLDER PEOPLE GROUP SUBSCRIPTION FORM

All our Bible reading notes can be ordered online
by visiting **brfonline.org.uk/collections/subscriptions**

The group subscription rate for *Bible Reflections for Older People* will be £15.45 per person until April 2021.

☐ I would like to take out a group subscription for .... (*quantity*) copies.

☐ Please start my order with the September 2020 / January 2021 / May 2021* issue.
I would like to pay annually/receive an invoice with each edition of the notes.* (**delete as appropriate*)

Please do not send any money with your order. Send your order to BRF and we will send you an invoice. The group subscription year is from 1 May to 30 April. If you start subscribing in the middle of a subscription year we will invoice you for the remaining number of issues left in that year.

Name and address of the person organising the group subscription:

Title .... First name/initials .... Surname..

Address...

.... Postcode ....

Telephone.................................... Email...

Church..

Name of minister ....

Name and address of the person paying the invoice if the invoice needs to be sent directly to them:

Title .... First name/initials .... Surname..

Address...

.... Postcode ....

Telephone.................................... Email...

Please return this form to:
BRF, 15 The Chambers, Vineyard, Abingdon OX14 3FE | enquiries@brf.org.uk
To read our terms and conditions, please visit **brfonline.org.uk/terms**.

The Bible Reading Fellowship is a Registered Charity (233280)

BIBLE REFLECTIONS FOR OLDER PEOPLE INDIVIDUAL/GIFT SUBSCRIPTION FORM

> To order online, please visit **brfonline.org.uk/collections/subscriptions**

☐ I would like to take out a subscription (*complete your name and address details only once*)
☐ I would like to give a gift subscription (*please provide both names and addresses*)

Title .... First name/initials .... Surname ....

Address ....

.... Postcode ....

Telephone .... Email ....

Gift subscription name ....

Gift subscription address ....

.... Postcode ....

Gift message (*20 words max. or include your own gift card*):

Please send *Bible Reflections for Older People* beginning with the September 2020 / January 2021 / May 2021* issue (**delete as appropriate*):

(*please tick box*)	UK	Europe	Rest of world
Bible Reflections for Older People	☐ £19.65	☐ £27.30	☐ £31.35

Total enclosed £ .... (*cheques should be made payable to 'BRF'*)

Please charge my MasterCard / Visa ☐ Debit card ☐ with £ ....

Card no. ☐☐☐☐ ☐☐☐☐ ☐☐☐☐ ☐☐☐☐

Expires end ☐☐ ☐☐   Security code* ☐☐☐   Last 3 digits on the reverse of the card

Signature* _____ Date ..../......./......

*ESSENTIAL IN ORDER TO PROCESS YOUR ORDER

Please return this form to:
BRF, 15 The Chambers, Vineyard, Abingdon OX14 3FE | enquiries@brf.org.uk
To read our terms and conditions, please visit **brfonline.org.uk/terms**.

BROP0220   The Bible Reading Fellowship is a Registered Charity (233280)